Knock-Knock Jokes

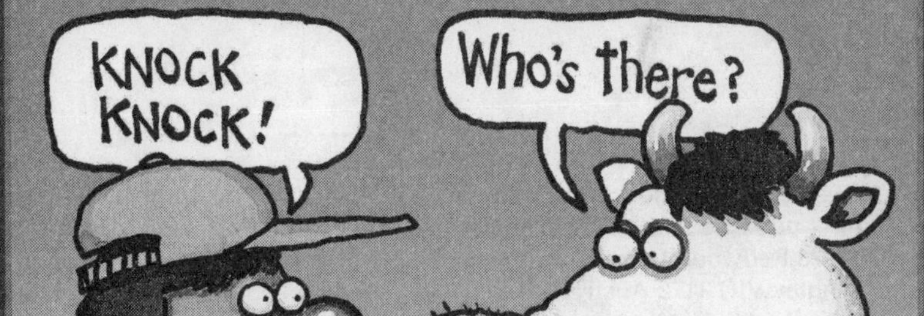

with Glen Singleton

Crazy Book of Knock Knock Jokes
First published in 2003 by Hinkler Books Pty Ltd
17–23 Redwood Drive
Dingley VIC 3172 Australia
www.hinklerbooks.com

ISBN: 1865156876

Cover designer: Peter Tovey Studios
Editor: Rose Inserra
Typesetting: Midland Typesetters
Printed and bound in Australia

Crazy Book of Knock Knock Jokes

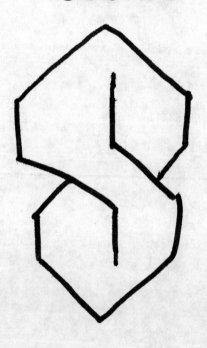

Knock Knock
Who's there?
Alison!
Alison who?
Alison to the radio!

Knock Knock
Who's there?
Ahmed!
Ahmed who?
Ahmed a mistake! I think I want the house next door!

Knock Knock
Who's there?
Avon!
Avon who?
Avon you to open the door!

1

Knock Knock
Who's there?
Avon!
Avon who?
Avon you to be my wife!

Knock Knock
Who's there?
Aida!
Aida who?
Aida whole box of cookies and now
I feel sick!

Knock Knock
Who's there?
Artichokes!
Artichokes who?
Artichokes when he eats too fast!

Knock Knock
Who's there?
Avenue!
Avenue who?
Avenue heard these jokes before?

Knock Knock
Who's there?
Avenue!
Avenue who?
Avenue got a doorbell?

Knock Knock
Who's there?
Army!
Army who?
Army and you still friends?

Knock Knock
Who's there?
Aitch!
Aitch who?
Bless you!

Knock Knock
Who's there?
Arch!
Arch who?
Bless you!

AAAARRCHOOO

Knock Knock
Who's there?
Alota!
Alota who?
Alota good this is doing me!

Knock Knock
Who's there?
Alaska!
Alaska who?
Alaska one more time. Let me in!

Knock Knock
Who's there?
Alaska!
Alaska who?
Alaska no questions! You tella no lies!

Knock Knock
Who's there?
Alf!
Alf who?
Alf all if you don't catch me!

Knock Knock

Who's there?

Alex!

Alex who?

Alexplain later, just let me in!

Knock Knock

Who's there?

Abbot!

Abbot who?

Abbot you don't know who this is!

Knock Knock

Who's there?

Accordion!

Accordion who?

Accordion to the TV, it's going to rain tomorrow!

Knock Knock
Who's there?
Amos!
Amos who?
Amosquito!

Knock Knock
Who's there?
Annather
~~Anna~~ *who?*
Annather mosquito!

Knock Knock
Who's there?
Adore!
Adore who?
Adore is between us, open up!

Knock Knock
Who's there?
Adore!
Adore who?
Adore is for knocking on!

Knock Knock
Who's there?
Arthur!
Arthur who?
Arthur anymore questions you have?

Knock Knock
Who's there?
Amiss!
Amiss who?
Amiss you! That's why I'm here!

Knock Knock
Who's there?
Ammonia!
Ammonia who?
Ammonia little girl
who can't reach the
door bell!

Knock Knock
Who's there?
Abe!
Abe who?
Abe C D E F G H!

Knock Knock
Who's there?
Abel!
Abel who?
Abel seaman!

Knock Knock
Who's there?
Attila!
Attila who?
Attila if you let me in!

Knock Knock
Who's there?
Arncha!
Arncha who?
Arncha going to let me in? It's freezing out here!

Knock Knock
Who's there?
Arthur!
Arthur who?
Arthur anymore jelly beans in the jar?

Knock Knock
Who's there?
Abba!
Abba who?
Abba banana!

Knock Knock
Who's there?
Abbey!
Abbey who?
Abbey stung me
on the nose!

Knock Knock
Who's there?
Abbey!
Abbey who?
Abbey hive is where honey is made!

Knock Knock
Who's there?
Armageddon!
Armageddon who?
Armageddon out of here!

Knock Knock
Who's there?
Adam!
Adam who?
Adam up and tell me the total!

Knock Knock
Who's there?
Alan!
Alan who?
Alan a good cause!

Knock Knock
Who's there?
A Fred!
A Fred who?
Who's a Fred of the Big Bad Wolf?

Knock Knock
Who's there?
Abbott! ·
Abbott who?
Abbott time you opened this door!

Knock Knock
Who's there?
Acute!
Acute who?
Acute little boy!

Knock Knock
Who's there?
Adder!
Adder who?
Adder you get in here?

Knock Knock
Who's there?
Aesop!
Aesop who?
Aesop I saw a puddy cat!

Knock Knock
Who's there?
Albert!
Albert who?
Albert you don't know who this is?

Knock Knock
Who's there?
Ahab!
Ahab who?
Ahab to go to the toilet now! Quick, open the door!

Knock Knock
Who's there?
Althea!
Althea who?
Althea later, alligator!

Knock Knock
Who's there?
Augusta!
Augusta who?
Augusta wind blew my hat away!

Knock Knock
Who's there?
Abyssinia!
Abyssina who?
Abyssinia when I get back!

Knock Knock
Who's there?
Adair!
Adair who?
Adair once, but
I'm bald now!

Knock Knock
Who's there?
Boo!
Boo who?
What are you crying about?

Knock Knock
Who's there?
Boo!
Boo who?
Here's a hanky, now let me in!

Knock Knock
Who's there?
Ben!
Ben who?
Ben knocking on the door all afternoon!

Knock Knock
Who's there?
Ben!
Ben who?
Ben down and look through the letter slot!

Knock Knock
Who's there?
Bab!
Bab who?
Baboons are a type of ape!

Knock Knock
Who's there?
Baby!
Baby who?
(sings) Baby, baby, baby ~~I love you!~~ ooooohhh

Knock Knock
Who's there?
Banana!
Banana who?
Banana split, so ice creamed!

Knock Knock
Who's there?
Bark!
Bark who?
Barking up the wrong tree!

Knock Knock
Who's there?
Butcher!
Butcher who?
Butcher little arms around me!

Knock Knock
Who's there?
Barry!
Barry who?
Barry the treasure where no one will find it!

Knock Knock
Who's there?
Bashful!
Bashful who?
I'm too shy to tell you!

Knock Knock
Who's there?
Bass!
Bass who?
Bass ball and softball are my favourite sports!

Knock Knock
Who's there?
Bat!
Bat who?
Bat you'll never guess!

Knock Knock
Who's there?
Bat!
Bat who?
Batman and Robin are superheroes!

Knock Knock
Who's there?
Bean!
Bean who?
Bean working too hard lately!

Knock Knock
Who's there?
Beck!
Beck who?
Beckfast is ready!

Knock Knock
Who's there?
Beet!
Beet who?
Beets me! I've forgotten my own name!

Knock Knock
Who's there?
Butcher!
Butcher who?
Butcher left leg in, butcher left leg out . . .

BUTCHER LEFT LEG IN
AND SHAKE IT
ALL ABOUT

Knock Knock
Who's there?
Bernadette!
Bernadette who?
Bernadette my lunch! Now I'm starving!

Knock Knock
Who's there?
Beryl!
Beryl who?
Roll out the Beryl!

Knock Knock
Who's there?
Bing!
Bing who?
Bingo starts in half an hour!

Knock Knock
Who's there?
Byra!
Byra who?
Byra light of the silvery moon!

Knock Knock
Who's there?
Bjorn!
Bjorn who?
Bjorn free!

Knock Knock
Who's there?
Bolton!
Bolton who?
Bolton the door! That's why I can't get in!

Knock Knock
Who's there?
Bear!
Bear who?
Bearer of glad tidings!

Knock Knock
Who's there?
Butcher!
Butcher who?
Butcher hand on the doorknob and let me in!

Knock Knock
Who's there?
Butcher!
Butcher who?
Butcher money where your mouth is!

Knock Knock
Who's there?
Bear!
Bear who?
Bear bum!

Knock Knock
Who's there?
Betty!
Betty who?
Betty late than never!

Knock Knock
Who's there?
Betty!
Betty who?
Betty let me in or they'll be trouble!

Knock Knock
Who's there?
Bach!
Bach who?
Bach of chips!

Knock Knock
Who's there?
Back!
Back who?
Back off, I'm going to force my way in!

Knock Knock
Who's there?
Bacon!
Bacon who?
Bacon a cake for your birthday!

Knock Knock
Who's there?
Bart!
Bart who?
Bartween you and me, I'm sick of standing in the cold!

Knock Knock
Who's there?
Bee!
Bee who?
Bee careful!

Knock Knock
Who's there?
Beef!
Beef who?
Bee fair now!

Knock Knock

Who's there?

Butter!

Butter who?

Butter wear a coat when you come out. It's cold!

Knock Knock

Who's there?

Brie!

Brie who?

Brie me my supper!

Knock Knock

Who's there?

Bassoon!

Bassoon who?

Bassoon things will be better!

Knock Knock
Who's there?
Bea!
Bea who?
Because I'm worth it!

Knock Knock
Who's there?
Barbie!
Barbie who?
Barbie Q!

Knock Knock
Who's there?
Beezer!
Beezer who?
Beezer black and yellow and make honey!

Knock Knock
Who's there?
Ben Hur!
Ben Hur who?
Ben Hur almost an hour so let me in!

Knock Knock
Who's there?
Beth!
Beth who?
Beth wisheth, thweetie!

Knock Knock
Who's there?
Beth!
Beth who?
Bethlehem is where Jesus was born!

Knock Knock
Who's there?
Burglar!
Burglar who?
Burglars don't knock!

Knock Knock
Who's there?
Baby Owl!
Baby Owl who?
Baby Owl see you later, maybe I won't!

Knock Knock
Who's there?
Barbara!
Barbara who?
Barbara black sheep, have you any wool …

Knock Knock
Who's there?
Bart!
Bart who?
Bart-enders serve drinks!

Knock Knock
Who's there?
Ben!
Ben who?
Ben away a long time!

Knock Knock
Who's there?
Biafra!
Biafra who?
Biafra'id, be very afraid!

Knock Knock
Who's there?
Boxer!
Boxer who?
Boxer tricks!

Knock Knock
Who's there?
Bowl!
Bowl who?
Bowl me over!

Knock Knock
Who's there?
Bea!
Bea who?
Because I said so!

Knock Knock
Who's there?
Bean!
Bean who?
Bean to any movies lately?

Knock Knock
Who's there?
Bella!
Bella who?
Bella bottom trousers!

KnockKnock
Who's there?
Cargo!
Cargo who?
Cargo beep beep!

Knock Knock
Who's there?
Caterpillar!
Caterpillar who?
Cat-er-pillar of feline society!

Knock Knock
Who's there?
Caitlin!
Caitlin who?
Caitlin you any more money. I'm broke!

Knock Knock
Who's there?
Catch!
Catch who?
God bless you!

Knock Knock
Who's there?
C-2!
C-2 who?
C-2 it that you remember me next time!

Knock Knock
Who's there?
Cameron!
Cameron who?
Cameron film are what you need to take pictures!

Knock Knock
Who's there?
Cornflakes!
Cornflakes who?
I'll tell you tomorrow, it's a cereal!

Knock Knock
Who's there?
Celia!
Celia who?
Celia later
alligator!

Knock Knock
Who's there?
Candice!
Candice who?
Candice get any better?

Knock Knock
Who's there?
Card!
Card who?
Card you see it's me?

Knock Knock
Who's there?
Carl!
Carl who?
Carload of furniture for you!
Where do you want it?

Knock Knock
Who's there?
Chuck!
Chuck who?
Chuck if I've left my keys inside!

Knock Knock
Who's there?
Carrie!
Carrie who?
Carrie on with what you're doing!

Knock Knock
Who's there?
Carson!
Carson who?
Carsonogenic!

Knock Knock
Who's there?
Cassie!
Cassie who?
Cassie through my fringe! I think
I need a haircut!

Knock Knock
Who's there?
Cassa!
Cassa who?
Cassablanca is my favourite movie!

Knock Knock
Who's there?
Closure!
Closure who?
Closure mouth when you're eating!

Knock Knock
Who's there?
Cher!
Cher who?
Cher and share alike!

Knock Knock
Who's there?
Chicken!
Chicken who?
Chicken your pocket! My keys
might be there!

Knock Knock
Who's there?
Claire!
Claire who?
Claire the snow from your path or someone will have an accident!

Knock Knock
Who's there?
Cologne!
Cologne who?
Cologne me names won't get you anywhere!

Knock Knock
Who's there?
Cosi!
Cosi who?
Cosi had to!

Knock Knock

Who's there?

Costas!

Costas who?

Costas a fortune to make the trip here!

Knock Knock

Who's there?

Crete!

Crete who?

Crete to be here!

Knock Knock

Who's there?

Crispin!

Crispin who?

Crispin juicy is how I like my chicken!

Knock Knock
Who's there?
Caesar!
Caesar who?
Caesar quickly, before she gets away!

Knock Knock
Who's there?
Carrie!
Carrie who?
Carrie me inside, I'm exhausted!

Knock Knock
Who's there?
Carlotta!
Carlotta who?
Carlotta trouble when it breaks down!

Knock Knock
Who's there?
Cantaloupe!
Cantaloupe who?
Cantaloupe with you tonight!

Knock Knock
Who's there?
Carmen!
Carmen who?
Carmen get it!

Knock Knock
Who's there?
Carol!
Carol who?
Carol go if you fill it with petrol!

Knock Knock
Who's there?
Cows!
Cows who?
Cows go 'moo', not 'who'!

Knock Knock
Who's there?
Cattle!
Cattle who?
Cattle always purr when you stroke it!

Knock Knock
Who's there?
Cecil!
Cecil who?
Cecil have music where ever she goes!

Knock Knock
Who's there?
Cash!
Cash who?
Are you a nut?

Knock Knock
Who's there?
Celeste!
Celeste who?
Celeste time I come round here!

Knock Knock
Who's there?
Colin!
Colin who?
Colin all cars! Colin all cars!

Knock Knock
Who's there?
Cheese!
Cheese who?
Cheese a jolly good fellow!

Knock Knock
Who's there?
Cook!
Cook who?
One o'clock!

Knock Knock
Who's there?
Curry!
Curry who?
Curry me back home please!

Knock Knock
Who's there?
Caesar!
Caesar who?
Caesar jolly good fellow!

Knock Knock
Who's there?
Canoe!
Canoe who?
Canoe come
out and play
with me?

Knock Knock
Who's there?
Dingo!
Dingo who?
Dingo anywhere on the weekend

Knock Knock
Who's there?
Dat!
Dat who?
Dat's all folks!

Knock Knock
Who's there?
Debate!
Debate who?
Debate goes on de hook if you want
to catch de fish!

Knock Knock
Who's there?
Dad!
Dad who?
Dad 2 and 2 to get 4!

Knock Knock
Who's there?
Dale!
Dale who?
Dale come if you ask dem!

Knock Knock
Who's there?
Data!
Data who?
Data remember!

Knock Knock
Who's there?
Deanna!
Deanna who?
Deanna-mals need feeding!

Knock Knock
Who's there?
Delores!
Delores who?
I fought Delores and Delores won!

Knock Knock
Who's there?
Dewayne!
Dewayne who?
Dewayne the bathtub before I drown!

Knock Knock
Who's there?
Denise!
Denise who?
Denise are between the waist
and the feet!

Knock Knock
Who's there?
Des!
Des who?
Des no bell! That's why I'm knocking!

Knock Knock
Who's there?
Diego!
Diego who?
Diegos before the B!

Knock Knock
Who's there?
Dish!
Dish who?
Dish is getting boring! Open the door!

Knock Knock
Who's there?
Despair!
Despair who?
Despair tyre is flat!

Knock Knock
Who's there?
Diss!
Diss who?
Diss is a recorded message! 'Knock Knock
Knock Knock Knock Knock.'

Knock Knock
Who's there?
Diss!
Diss who?
Diss is ridiculous! Let me in!

Knock Knock
Who's there?
Disguise!
Disguise who?
Disguise the limit!

Knock Knock
Who's there?
Diesel!
Diesel who?
Diesel help with your cold! Take two
every four hours!

Knock Knock
Who's there?
Doctor!
Doctor who?
That's right!

Knock Knock
Who's there?
Don!
Don who?
Don just stand there! Open the door!

Knock Knock
Who's there?
Don!
Don who?
(shouts) Don-key rides! Donkey rides!
Only five dollars a ride!

Knock Knock
Who's there?
Duncan!
Duncan who?
Duncan disorderly!

Knock Knock
Who's there?
Dishes!
Dishes who?
Dishes a very bad joke!

Knock Knock
Who's there?
Dan!
Dan who?
Dan Druff!

Knock Knock
Who's there?
Danielle!
Danielle who?
Danielle so loud, I can hear you!

Knock Knock
Who's there?
Daryl!
Daryl who?
Daryl never be another you!

Knock Knock
Who's there?
Dave!
Dave who?
Dave-andalised our house!

Knock Knock
Who's there?
Datsun!
Datsun who?
Datsun old joke!

Knock Knock
Who's there?
Doris!
Doris who?
The Doris locked so let me in!

Knock Knock
Who's there?
Dozen!
Dozen who?
Dozen anyone know who I am?

Knock Knock
Who's there?
Dish!
Dish who?
Dish is a stick-up!

Knock Knock
Who's there?
Eiffel!
Eiffel who?
Eiffel down!

Knock Knock
Who's there?
Euripedes!
Euripedes who?
Euripedes pants, Eumenides pants!

Knock Knock
Who's there?
Empty!
Empty who?
Empty V (MTV)!

Knock Knock
Who's there?
Eddie!
Eddie who?
Eddie body home?

Knock Knock
Who's there?
Eel!
Eel who?
(sings) Eel meet again, don't know where,
don't know when!

KnockKnock
Who's there?
Eamon!
Eamon who?
Eamon a really good mood!

Knock Knock
Who's there?
Eight!
Eight who?
Eight my lunch too quickly!
Now I've got a stomach ache!

Knock Knock
Who's there?
Elizabeth!
Elizabeth who?
Elizabeth of love goes a long way!

Knock Knock
Who's there?
Ears!
Ears who?
Ears some more knock knock jokes!

Knock Knock
Who's there?
Ella!
Ella who?
Ella-mentary, my dear fellow!

Knock Knock
Who's there?
Ellie!
Ellie who?
Ellie-phants never forget!

Knock Knock
Who's there?
Ellis!
Ellis who?
Ellis between K and M!

Knock Knock
Who's there?
Elsie!
Elsie who?
Elsie you down at the mall!

Knock Knock
Who's there?
Emil!
Emil who?
Emil fit for a king!

Knock Knock
Who's there?
Eugene!
Eugene who?
Eugene, me Tarzan!

Knock Knock
Who's there?
Europe!
Europe who?
Europen the door so I can come in!

Knock Knock
Who's there?
Effie!
Effie who?
Effie'd known you were coming he'd have stayed at home!

Knock Knock
Who's there?
Evan!
Evan who?
I'm Knock Knock, knocking on Evan's door!

Knock Knock
Who's there?
Eye!
Eye who?
Eye know who you are! Don't you know
who I am?

Knock Knock
Who's there?
Eliza!
Eliza who?
Eliza wake at night thinking about you!

Knock Knock
Who's there?
Evan!
Evan who?
Evan you should know who I am!

Knock Knock
Who's there?
Eileen!
Eileen who?
Eileen to the left because one leg is shorter than the other!

Knock Knock
Who's there?
Freeze!
Freeze who?
Freeze a jolly good fellow!

Knock Knock
Who's there?
Fantasy!
Fantasy who?
Fantasy a walk on the beach!

Knock Knock
Who's there?
Ferdie!
Ferdie who?
Ferdie last time open the door!

Knock Knock
Who's there?
Fanny!
Fanny who?
Fanny the way you keep asking Who's there?'

Knock Knock
Who's there?
Figs!
Figs who?
Figs the doorbell, it's been broken for ages!

Knock Knock
Who's there?
Fido!
Fido who?
Fido known you were going to be like this
I would have brought my key!

Knock Knock
Who's there?
Fitzsimon!
Fitzsimon who?
Fitzsimon better than it fits me!

Knock Knock
Who's there?
Flea!
Flea who?
Flea thirty is when I've got to be home!

Knock Knock
Who's there?
Fly!
Fly who?
Fly away Peter, fly away Paul!

Knock Knock
Who's there?
Foster!
Foster who?
Foster than a speeding bullet!

Knock Knock
Who's there?
Francis!
Francis who?
Francis is the home of the Eiffel Tower!

Knock Knock
Who's there?
Frank!
Frank who?
Frankly my dear, I
don't give a damn!

Knock Knock
Who's there?
Felix!
Felix who?
Felix my ice-cream
I'll lick his!

71

Knock Knock
Who's there?
Fang!
Fang who?
Fangs for opening the door!

Knock Knock
Who's there?
Fred!
Fred who?
I'm a Fred of the dark!

Knock Knock
Who's there?
Fozzie!
Fozzie who?
Fozzie hundredth time, my name is Nick!

Knock Knock
Who's there?
Gotter!
Gotter who?
Gotter go to the toilet!

Knock Knock
Who's there?
Gladys!
Gladys who?
Gladys Saturday aren't you?

Knock Knock
Who's there?
German border patrol
German border patrol who?
Ve vill ask ze questions!

Knock Knock
Who's there?
Gable!
Gable who?
Gable to leap tall buildings in a single bound!

Knock Knock
Who's there?
Galahad!
Galahad who?
Galahad a sore leg, so he couldn't come!

Knock Knock
Who's there?
Gary!
Gary who?
Gary on smiling!

Knock Knock
Who's there?
Genoa!
Genoa who?
Genoa good place to have a
meal around here?

Knock Knock
Who's there?
Germaine!
Germaine who?
Germaine you don't recognise me?

Knock Knock
Who's there?
Gene!
Gene who?
Genealogy is the study of family trees!

Knock Knock
Who's there?
Goose!
Goose who?
Goosey Goosey Gander!

Knock Knock
Who's there?
Gopher!
Gopher who?
Gopher help, I've been tied up!

Knock Knock
Who's there?
Gorilla!
Gorilla who?
Gorilla cheese sandwich for me, please!

Knock Knock
Who's there?
Guinea!
Guinea who?
Guinea some money so I can buy some food!

Knock Knock
Who's there?
Gus!
Gus who?
No, you guess who. I already know!

Knock Knock
Who's there?
Guthrie!
Guthrie who?
Guthrie musketeers!

Knock Knock
Who's there?
Grant!
Grant who?
Grant you three wishes!

Knock Knock
Who's there?
Gizza!
Gizza who?
Gizza kiss!

kissy
kissy
kissy

Knock Knock
Who's there?
Gwen!
Gwen who?
Gwen will I see you again?

Knock Knock
Who's there?
Galway!
Galway who?
Galway, you're annoying me!

Knock Knock
Who's there?
Germany!
Germany who?
Germany people knock on your door?

Knock Knock
Who's there?
Harley!
Harley who?
Harley ever see you anymore!

Knock Knock
Who's there?
Howard!
Howard who?
Howard I know?

Knock Knock
Who's there?
Hacienda!
Hacienda who?
Hacienda the story! It's bedtime now!

Knock Knock
Who's there?
Haden!
Haden who?
Haden seek!

Knock Knock
Who's there?
Hair!
Hair who?
I'm hair to stay!

Knock Knock
Who's there?
Halibut!
Halibut who?
Halibut letting me in!

Knock Knock
Who's there?
Hal!
Hal who?
Hello to you too!

Knock Knock
Who's there?
Hal!
Hal who?
Hallelujah!

Knock Knock
Who's there?
Haley!
Haley who?
Haley-ions come from outer space!

Knock Knock
Who's there?
Hammond!
Hammond who?
Hammond eggs for breakfast please!

Knock Knock
Who's there?
Hans!
Hans who?
Hans are on the end of your arms!

Knock Knock
Who's there?
Harlow!
Harlow who?
Harlow Dolly!

Knock Knock
Who's there?
Harmony!
Harmony who?
Harmony electricians does it take
to change a lightbulb?

Knock Knock
Who's there?
Harp!
Harp who?
Harpoon the whales!

Knock Knock
Who's there?
Havana!
Havana who?
Havana great time!

Knock Knock
Who's there?
Havalock!
Havalock who?
Havalock put on your door!

Knock Knock
Who's there?
Heidi!
Heidi who?
Heidi ho!

Knock Knock
Who's there?
Hester!
Hester who?
Hester la vista!

Knock Knock
Who's there?
Hey!
Hey who?
Hey ho, hey ho, it's off to work we go!

Knock Knock
Who's there?
Hijack!
Hijack who?
Hi jack! Where's Jill?

Knock Knock
Who's there?
House!
House who?
House it going?

Knock Knock
Who's there?
Holmes!
Holmes who?
Holmes sweet home!

Knock Knock
Who's there?
Howdy!
Howdy who?
Howdy do that?

Knock Knock
Who's there?
Haywood, Hugh and Harry!
Haywood, Hugh and Harry who?
Haywood, Hugh, Harry up and open
the door!

Knock Knock
Who's there?
Hugo!
Hugo who?
Hugo one way, I'll go the other!

Knock Knock
Who's there?
Hosanna!
Hosanna who?
Hosanna Claus delivers all those presents,
I'll never know!

Knock Knock
Who's there?
Ida!
Ida who?
Ida hard time getting here!

Knock Knock
Who's there?
Ike!
Ike who?
(sings) Ike could have danced all night!

Knock Knock
Who's there?
Ima!
Ima who?
Ima going to home if you don't let me in!

Knock Knock
Who's there?
Ines!
Ines who?
Ines second I'm going to turn around
and go home!

Knock Knock
Who's there?
Iran!
Iran who?
Iran ten laps
around the track
and I'm very tired
now!

Knock Knock
Who's there?
Ira!
Ira who?
Ira-te if you don't let me in!

Knock Knock
Who's there?
Ivan!
Ivan who?
No, Ivanhoe!

Knock Knock
Who's there?
Icon!
Icon who?
Icon tell you another Knock Knock joke!
Do you want me to?

Knock Knock
Who's there?
Ice-cream!
Ice-cream who?
Ice cream, you scream!

Knock Knock
Who's there?
Ice cream soda!
Ice cream soda who?
Ice cream soda neighbours wake up!

Knock Knock
Who's there?
Icy!
Icy who?
I see your underwear!

Knock Knock
Who's there?
Irish!
Irish who?
Irish I had a million dollars!

Knock Knock
Who's there ?
Irish stew!
Irish stew who?
Irish stew in the name of the law!

Knock Knock
Who's there?
Ida!
Ida who?
(sings) Ida know why I love you like I do!

Knock Knock
Who's there?
Igloo!
Igloo who?
(sings) Igloo knew Suzie like I know Suzie!

Knock Knock
Who's there?
Ivor!
Ivor who?
Ivor you let me in or I'll break the
door down!

Knock Knock!
Who's there?
Irish!
Irish who?
Irish I knew some more Knock Knock jokes

Knock Knock
Who's there?
Jamaica!
Jamaica who?
Jamaica mistake!

Knock Knock
Who's there?
Jam!
Jam who?
Jam mind, I'm trying to get out!

Knock Knock
Who's there?
James!
James who?
James people play!

Knock Knock
Who's there?
Jilly!
Jilly who?
Jilly out here, so let me in!

Knock Knock
Who's there?
Jack!
Jack who?
Jack pot! You're a winner!

Knock Knock
Who's there?
Jack!
Jack who?
Jack of all trades!

Knock Knock
Who's there?
Jasmine!
Jasmine who?
Jasmine play the saxophone, piano
and trumpet!

Knock Knock
Who's there?
Jean!
Jean who?
Jean-ius! Ask me a question!

Knock Knock
Who's there?
Justin!
Justin who?
Justin time for lunch!

Knock Knock
Who's there?
Jerry!
Jerry who?
Jerry can, even if you can't!

Knock Knock
Who's there?
Jess!
Jess who?
Jess me and my shadow!

Knock Knock
Who's there?
Jester!
Jester who?
Jester minute! I'm looking for my key!

Knock Knock
Who's there?
Jethro!
Jethro who?
Jethro a rope out the window!

Knock Knock
Who's there?
Jewell!
Jewell who?
Jewell know me when you see me!

Knock Knock
Who's there?
Joan!
Joan who?
Joan call us, we'll call you!

Knock Knock
Who's there?
Juan!
Juan who?
Juan to come out and play?

Knock Knock
Who's there?
Juan!
Juan who?
(sings) Juan two three o'clock,
four o'clock rock!

Knock Knock
Who's there?
Jaws!
Jaws who?
Jaws truly!

Knock Knock
Who's there?
Juice!
Juice who?
Juice still want to know?

Knock Knock
Who's there?
July!
July who?
July and your nose will grow!

Knock Knock
Who's there?
Juno!
Juno who?
I know who, do you know who?

Knock Knock
Who's there?
Justice!
Justice who?
Justice I thought! You won't let me in!

Knock Knock
Who's there?
Jimmy!
Jimmy who?
Jimmy a little kiss on the cheek!

Knock Knock
Who's there?
Jo!
Jo who?
Jo jump in the lake!

Knock Knock
Who's there?
Java!
Java who?
Java dollar you can lend me?

Knock Knock
Who's there?
Jeff!
Jeff who?
Jeff in one ear, can you please speak
a bit louder!

Knock Knock
Who's there?
Jim!
Jim who?
Jim mind if we
come in!

Knock Knock
Who's there?
Kenya!
Kenya who?
Kenya keep the noise down,
some of us are trying to sleep!

Knock Knock
Who's there?
Knee!
Knee who?
Knee-d you ask?

Knock Knock
Who's there?
Knock Knock
Who's there?
Knock Knock
Who's there?
I'm sorry, but Mum told me never
to speak to strangers!

Knock Knock
Who's there?
Kay!
Kay who?
Kay sera sera!

Knock Knock
Who's there?
Kanga!
Kango who?
No, kangaroo!

Knock Knock
Who's there?
Kareem!
Kareem who?
Kareem rises to the surface!

Knock Knock
Who's there?
Kendall!
Kendall who?
Kendall is Barbie's friend!

Knock Knock
Who's there?
Kent!
Kent who?
Kent you let me in?

Knock Knock
Who's there?
Ken!
Ken who?
Ken I come in, it's freezing out here!

Knock Knock
Who's there?
Kermit!
Kermit who?
Kermit a crime and you'll go to jail!

Knock Knock
Who's there?
Kim!
Kim who?
Kim too late by the look of it!

Knock Knock
Who's there?
Kipper!
Kipper who?
Kipper your hands off me!

Knock Knock
Who's there?
Lettuce!
Lettuce who?
Lett-uce in, it's cold outside!

Knock Knock
Who's there?
Lauren!
Lauren who?
Lauren order!

Knock Knock
Who's there?
Laziness!
Laziness who?
Laziness bed all day! I don't
know what to do!

Knock Knock
Who's there?
Lee King!
Lee King who?
Lee King bucket!

Knock Knock
Who's there?
Luke!
Luke who?
Luke through the
peephole and
you'll see!

Knock Knock
Who's there?
Len!
Len who?
Len me some money!

Knock Knock
Who's there?
Leonie!
Leonie who?
Leonie one for me!

Knock Knock
Who's there?
Les!
Les who?
Les go out for dinner!

Knock Knock
Who's there?
Lillian!
Lillian who?
Lillian the garden!

Knock Knock
Who's there?
Lionel!
Lionel who?
Lionel bite you
if you don't
watch out!

Knock Knock
Who's there?
Lion!
Lion who?
Lion down is the best thing to do when
you're sick!

Knock Knock
Who's there?
Leif !
Leif who?
Leif me alone!

Knock Knock
Who's there?
Lois!
Lois who?
Lois the opposite of high!

Knock Knock
Who's there?
Lon!
Lon who?
Lon ago, in a land far, far away . . .

Knock Knock
Who's there?
Lotte!
Lotte who?
Lotte people wouldn't treat me
the way you do!

Knock Knock
Who's there?
Lucinda!
Lucinda who?
(sings) Lucinda in the sky with diamonds!

Knock Knock
Who's there?
Lucy!
Lucy who?
Lucy lastic is embarrassing!

Knock Knock
Who's there?
Lass!
Lass who?
Are you a cowboy?

Knock Knock
Who's there?
Lisa!
Lisa who?
Lisa new car, furniture or computer
equipment!

Knock Knock
Who's there?
Lena!
Lena who?
Lena little closer and I'll tell you!

Knock Knock
Who's there?
Larva!
Larva who?
I larva you!

Knock Knock
Who's there?
Liz!
Liz who?
Lizen carefully to what I have to say!

Knock Knock
Who's there?
Little old lady!
Little old lady who?
I didn't know you could yodel!

Knock Knock
Who's there?
Letter!
Letter who?
Letter in or she'll knock the door down!

Knock Knock
Who's there?
Lie!
Lie who?
Lie low until the cops leave!

Knock Knock
Who's there?
Minnie!
Minnie who?
Minnie people would like to know!

Knock Knock
Who's there?
Midas!
Midas who?
Midas well let me in!

Knock Knock!
Who's there?
Max!
Max who?
Max no difference who it is – just open the door!

Knock Knock
Who's there?
May!
May who?
Maybe I'll tell you, maybe I won't!

Knock Knock
Who's there?
Maia!
Maia who?
Maiaunt and uncle are coming to stay!

Knock Knock
Who's there?
Malcolm!
Malcolm who?
Malcolm you won't
open the door?

Knock Knock
Who's there?
Mister!
Mister who?
Mister last train
home!

Knock Knock
Who's there?
Manny!
Manny who?
Manny are called, few are chosen!

Knock Knock
Who's there?
Mira!
Mira who?
Mira, Mira on the wall!

Knock Knock
Who's there?
Marcella!
Marcella who?
Marcella is damp and cold!

Knock Knock
Who's there?
Marie!
Marie who?
Marie the one you love!

Knock Knock
Who's there?
Martha!
Martha who?
Martha up to the top of the hill and
marched them down again!

Knock Knock
Who's there?
Mary!
Mary who?
Mary Christmas and a happy new year!

Knock Knock
Who's there?
Matt!
Matt who?
Matter of fact!

Knock Knock
Who's there?
Matthew!
Matthew who?
Matthew lace has
come undone!

Knock Knock
Who's there?
Miniature!
Miniature who?
Miniature let me
in I'll tell you!

Knock Knock
Who's there?
Moira!
Moira who?
The Moria merrier!

Knock Knock
Who's there?
Maude!
Maude who?
Mauden my life's worth!

Knock Knock
Who's there?
Mayonaisse!
Mayonaisse who?
Mayonaisse are hurting!
I think I need glasses!

Knock Knock
Who's there?
Meg!
Meg who?
Meg up your own mind!

Knock Knock
Who's there?
Mickey!
Mickey who?
Mickey is stuck in the lock!

Knock Knock
Who's there?
Mike and Angelo!
Mike and Angelo who?
Mike and Angelo was a great sculptor!

Knock Knock
Who's there?
Moppet!
Moppet who?
Moppet up before someone slips!

Knock Knock
Who's there?
Mortimer!
Mortimer who?
Mortimer than meets the eyes!

Knock Knock
Who's there?
Madam!
Madam who?
Madam foot got stuck in the door!

Knock Knock
Who's there?
Major!
Major who?
Major answer a Knock Knock joke!

Knock Knock
Who's there?
Mandy!
Mandy who?
Mandy lifeboats, we're sinking!

Knock Knock
Who's there?
Mabel!
Mabel who?
Mabel doesn't work either!

Knock Knock
Who's there?
Moira!
Moira who?
(sings) Moira see you, Moira want you!

Knock Knock
Who's there?
Mary Lee!
Mary Lee who?
(sings) Mary Lee, Mary Lee, Mary Lee,
Mary Lee, life is but a dream!

Knock Knock
Who's there?
Nest!
Nest who?
Nest time I'm going to ring before I come!

Knock Knock
Who's there?
Nero!
Nero who?
Nero far!

Knock Knock
Who's there?
Noah!
Noah who?
Noah good place for a meal?

Knock Knock
Who's there?
Norma Lee!
Norma Lee who?
Norma Lee I'd be at school but
I've got the day off!

Knock Knock
Who's there?
Noah!
Noah who?
Noah counting for taste!

Knock Knock
Who's there?
Noah!
Noah who?
Noah yes? What's your decision?

Knock Knock
Who's there?
Noise!
Noise who?
Noise to see you!

Knock Knock
Who's there?
Norway!
Norway who?
Norway am I leaving until
I've spoken to you!

Knock Knock
Who's there?
Nanna!
Nanna who?
Nanna your business!

There are hundreds of perfectly good banks to rob... you great brute... ...so buzz off!

Knock Knock
Who's there?
Nose!
Nose who?
Nosey parker! Mind your
own business!

Knock Knock
Who's there?
Nobel!
Nobel who?
No bell so I just knocked!

Knock Knock
Who's there?
Nobody!
Nobody who?
Just nobody!

Knock Knock
Who's there?
Neil!
Neil who?
Neil down and take a look through
the letter slot!

Knock Knock
Who's there?
Nicholas!
Nicholas who?
Nicholas girls shouldn't climb trees!

Knock Knock
Who's there?
Nobody!
Nobody who?
No body, just a skeleton!

Knock Knock
Who's there?
Orson!
Orson who?
Orson cart!

Knock Knock
Who's there?
Oscar!
Oscar who?
Oscar silly question get a silly answer!

Knock Knock
Who's there?
Olive!
Olive who?
Olive you!

Knock Knock
Who's there?
Offer!
Offer who?
Offer gotten who I am!

Knock Knock
Who's there?
Olive!
Olive Who?
Olive in that house across the road!

Knock Knock
Who's there?
Olivia!
Olivia who?
Olivia but I've lost my key!

Knock Knock
Who's there?
Oboe!
Oboe who?
Oboe, I've got the wrong house!

Knock Knock
Who's there?
Ohio!
Ohio who?
Ohio Silver!

Knock Knock
Who's there?
Omar!
Omar who?
Omar goodness gracious, I've got the wrong address!

Knock Knock
Who's there?
Oil!
Oil who?
Oil be seeing you!

Knock Knock
Who's there?
Oily!
Oily who?
The oily bird catches the worm!

Knock Knock
Who's there?
Ooze!
Ooze who?
Ooze in charge around here!

Knock Knock
Who's there?
Ocelot!
Ocelot who?
Ocelot of questions, don't you?

Knock Knock
Who's there?
Odysseus!
Odysseus who?
Odysseus the last straw!

Knock Knock
Who's there?
Ole!
Ole who?
Ole King Cole, I'm a merry old soul!

Knock Knock
Who's there?
Olga!
Olga who?
Olga way if you don't let me in!

Knock Knock
Who's there?
Omega!
Omega who?
Omega best man win!

Knock Knock
Who's there?
Ogre!
Ogre who?
Ogre the hill and far away!

Knock Knock
Who's there?
Onya!
Onya who?
Onya marks, get set, go!

Knock Knock
Who's there?
Oppa!
Oppa who?
Oppa-tunity knocks!

Knock Knock!
Who's there?
Pencil!
Pencil who?
If you don't wear suspenders your pencil
fall down!

Knock Knock
Who's there?
Phyllis!
Phyllis who?
Phyllis a glass of water will you!

Knock Knock
Who's there?
Passion!
Passion who?
Just passion by and I thought
I'd say hello!

Knock Knock
Who's there?
Patrick!
Patrick who?
Patricked me into coming over!

Knock Knock
Who's there?
P!
P who?
(shouts) P nuts, P nuts, get your
fresh P nuts!

Knock Knock
Who's there?
Paine!
Paine who?
Paine in my
stomach! I
need some
medicine!

Knock Knock
Who's there?
Police!
Police who?
Police let me in!

Knock Knock
Who's there?
Pa!
Pa who?
Pa-don me! Can I come in?

Knock Knock
Who's there?
Pa!
Pa who?
Pa-tridge in a pear tree!

Knock Knock
Who's there?
Parish!
Parish who?
Parish is the capital of France!

Knock Knock
Who's there?
Parsley!
Parsley who?
Parsley mustard please!

Knock Knock
Who's there?
Pasture!
Pasture who?
Pasture bedtime, isn't it?

Knock Knock
Who's there?
Patty!
Patty who?
Patty cake, patty cake, baker's man!

Knock Knock

Who's there?

Paul!

Paul who?

Paul thing! Let me in and I'll comfort you!

Knock Knock

Who's there?

Packer!

Packer who?

Packer your troubles in your old kit bag!

Umm.... that LOOSE PANTS DIET certainly works

Knock Knock

Who's there?

Panther!

Panther who?

My panther falling down!

Knock Knock
Who's there?
Paula!
Paula who?
Paula nother one! It's got bells on it!

Knock Knock
Who's there?
Pear!
Pear who?
Pear of freeloaders out here
wanting some dinner!

Knock Knock
Who's there?
Pecan!
Pecan who?
Pecan someone your own size!

Knock Knock
Who's there?
Percy!
Percy who?
Percy vere and you'll go a long way!

Knock Knock
Who's there?
Phil!
Phil who?
Phil my glass up to the rim!

Knock Knock
Who's there?
Phone!
Phone who?
Phone I'd known you wouldn't let me in,
I'd never have come!

Knock Knock
Who's there?
Pier!
Pier who?
Pier through the peephole and you'll see!

Knock Knock
Who's there?
Pinza!
Pinza who?
Pinza needles!

Knock Knock
Who's there?
Polly!
Polly who?
Polly put the kettle on! I'm dying
for a cup of tea!

Knock Knock
Who's there?
Poker!
Poker who?
Poker and see if she'll wake up!

Knock Knock
Who's there?
Quacker!
Quacker who?
Quacker 'nother bad joke and I'm leaving!

Knock Knock
Who's there?
Roach!
Roach who?
Roach you a letter but I didn't send it!

Knock Knock
Who's there?
Rabbit!
Rabbit who?
Rabbit up carefully, it's a present!

Knock Knock
Who's there?
Raoul!
Raoul who?
Raoul with the punches!

Knock Knock
Who's there?
Reed!
Reed who?
Reed-turn to sender!

Knock Knock
Who's there?
Renata!
Renata who?
Renata milk, can you spare a cup?

Knock Knock
Who's there?
Robin!
Robin who?
Robin you, so hand over your cash!

Knock Knock
Who's there?
Robin!
Robin who?
Robin the rich to give to the poor!

Knock Knock
Who's there?
Ringo!
Ringo who?
Ringo, Ringo roses!

Knock Knock
Who's there?
Roach!
Roach who?
Roach out, I'll be there!

Knock Knock
Who's there?
Rocky!
Rocky who?
Rocky bye baby on the tree top!

Knock Knock
Who's there?
Ron!
Ron who?
Ron house. Sorry for bothering you!

Knock Knock
Who's there?
Rosa!
Rosa who?
Rosa my favourite flowers!

Knock Knock
Who's there?
Rufus!
Rufus who?
Rufus leaking. I've come to fix it!

Knock Knock
Who's there?
Russell!
Russell who?
Russell up something to eat please!

Knock Knock
Who's there?
Russian!
Russian who?
Russian around all day.
Now I'm exhausted!

Knock Knock
Who's there?
Radio!
Radio Who?
Radio not, here I come!

Knock Knock
Who's there?
Ralph!
Ralph who?
Ralph! Ralph! Ralph! I'm a dog!

Knock Knock
Who's there?
Razor!
Razor who?
Razor hands, this is a stick up!

Knock Knock
Who's there?
Red!
Red who?
Knock Knock
Who's there?
Red!
Red who?
Knock Knock
Who's there?
Red!
Red who?
Knock Knock
Who's there?
Red!
Red who?
Knock Knock
Who's there?
Orange!
Orange who?
Orange you glad I didn't say red?

Knock Knock
Who's there?
Rhoda!
Rhoda who?
(sings) Row, Row, Rhoda boat!

Knock Knock
Who's there?
Rose!
Rose who?
Rose early to come and see you!

Knock Knock
Who's there?
Roxanne!
Roxanne who?
Roxanne pebbles are all over your garden!

Knock Knock
Who's there?
Sawyer!
Sawyer who?
Sawyer lights on thought I'd drop by!

Knock Knock
Who's there?
Scott!
Scott who?
Scott nothing to do with you!

Knock Knock
Who's there?
Shelby!
Shelby who?
Shelby comin' round the mountain
when she comes!

Knock Knock
Who's there?
Still!
Still who?
Still knocking!

Knock Knock
Who's there?
Shamp!
Shamp who?
Why, do I have lice?

Knock Knock!
Who's there?
Stopwatch!
Stopwatch who?
Stopwatch your doing and open this door!

Knock Knock
Who's there?
Sancho!
Sancho who?
Sancho a letter but you never answered!

Knock Knock
Who's there?
Snow!
Snow who?
Snow good asking me!

Knock Knock
Who's there?
Satin!
Satin who?
Who satin my chair!

Knock Knock
Who's there?
Stitch!
Stitch who?
Stitch in time saves nine!

Knock Knock
Who's there?
Sabina!
Sabina who?
Sabina long time since I've been
at your place!

Knock Knock
Who's there?
Sacha!
Sacha who?
Sacha fuss you're making!

Knock Knock
Who's there?
Sal!
Sal who?
Sal long way for me to go home!

Knock Knock
Who's there?
Sally!
Sally who?
Sally days yet!

Knock Knock
Who's there?
Sam!
Sam who?
Sam I am, green eggs and ham!

Knock Knock
Who's there?
Samantha!
Samantha who?
Samantha others have already gone!

Knock Knock
Who's there?
Smore!
Smore who?
Can I have smore marshmallows?

Knock Knock
Who's there?
Sarah!
Sarah who?
Sarah nother way in?

Knock Knock
Who's there?
Sari!
Sari who?
Sari I took so long!

Knock Knock
Who's there?
Says!
Says who?
Says me!

Knock Knock
Who's there?
Scold!
Scold who?
Scold out here, let me in!

eet eez such a love-el-ly day..... eet makes me want to sing

Knock Knock
Who's there?
Sombrero!
Sombrero who?
(sings)
Sombrero-ver
the rainbow!

Knock Knock
Who's there?
Sharon!
Sharon who?
Sharon share alike!

Knock Knock
Who's there?
Sherwood!
Sherwood who?
Sherwood love to come inside!
How about it?

Knock Knock
Who's there?
Shirley!
Shirley who?
Shirley you know by now!

Knock Knock
Who's there?
Simon!
Simon who?
Simon the dotted line and you
can have the parcel!

Knock Knock
Who's there?
Sam!
Sam who?
Sam person who knocked a minute ago!

Knock Knock
Who's there?
Sarah!
Sarah who?
Sarah doctor in the house?
I don't feel so good!

Knock Knock
Who's there?
Sibyl!
Sibyl who?
Sibyl Simon met a pieman going to the fair!

Knock Knock
Who's there?
Sigrid!
Sigrid who?
Sigrid Service, now do exactly as I say!

Knock Knock
Who's there?
Seymour!
Seymour who?
You'll Seymour if you look through the window!

Knock Knock
Who's there?
Spell!
Spell who?
W!H!O!

Knock Knock
Who's there?
Stan!
Stan who?
Stan back! I'm going to
break the door down!

Knock Knock
Who's there?
Tank!
Tank who?
You're welcome!

Knock Knock
Who's there?
Turnip!
Turnip who?
Turnip for school tomorrow or
there will be trouble!

Knock Knock
Who's there?
Turnip!
Turnip who?
Turn up the heater, it's cold in here!

Knock Knock
Who's there?
Tick!
Tick who?
Tick 'em up, I'm a tongue tied towboy!

Knock Knock
Who's there?
Troy!
Troy who?
Troy as I may I can't
reach the bell!

Knock Knock
Who's there?
Theresa!
Theresa who?
Theresa green!

Knock Knock
Who's there?
Tex!
Tex who?
Tex two to tango!

Knock Knock
Who's there?
Thistle!
Thistle who?
Thistle be the last time I knock

Knock Knock
Who's there?
Tibet!
Tibet who?
Early Tibet, early to rise!

Knock Knock
Who's there?
Tamara!
Tamara who?
Tamara is Wednesday, today is Tuesday!

Knock Knock
Who's there?
Tish!
Tish who?
Bless you!

Knock Knock
Who's there?
Tennis!
Tennis who?
Tennis five plus five!

Knock Knock
Who's there?
Teresa!
Teresa who?
Teresa green, the sky is blue!

Knock Knock
Who's there?
Teddy!
Teddy who?
Teddy the neighbourhood,
tomorrow the world!

Knock Knock
Who's there?
Tex!
Tex who?
Tex one to know one!

Knock Knock
Who's there?
Thumb!
Thumb who?
Thumb people would just let me in!

Knock Knock
Who's there?
Toes!
Toes who?
(sings) Toes were the days, my friend!

Knock Knock
Who's there?
Tom Sawyer!
Tom Sawyer who?
Tom Sawyer wagging school!

Knock Knock
Who's there?
Tommy!
Tommy who?
Tommy you love me!

Knock Knock
Who's there?
Tuba!
Tuba who?
Tuba toothpaste!

Knock Knock
Who's there?
Tooth!
Tooth who?
Tooth or dare!

Knock Knock
Who's there?
Toucan!
Toucan who?
Toucan play at this game!

Knock Knock
Who's there?
Toyota!
Toyota who?
Toyota be a law against Knock Knock jokes!

Knock Knock
Who's there?
Turner!
Turner who?
Turner round and you'll get a better look!

Knock Knock
Who's there?
The Sultan!
The Sultan who?
The Sultan Pepper!

Knock Knock
Who's there?
U-!
U- who?
U- can buy a brand new car, for only $199 a month!

Knock Knock
Who's there?
U-!
U- who?
U for me and me for you!

Knock Knock
Who's there?
Una!
Una who?
No I don't, tell me!

Knock Knock
Who's there?
U-8!
U- who?
U-8 my lunch!

Knock Knock
Who's there?
Utah!
Utah who?
Utahs the road and I'll mend the fence!

Knock Knock
Who's there?
Vitamin!
Vitamin who?
Vitam in for a party!

Knock Knock
Who's there?
Venice!
Venice who?
Venice your doorbell going to be fixed!

Knock Knock
Who's there?
Viola!
Viola who?
Viola sudden your bell doesn't work?

Knock Knock
Who's there?
Voodoo!
Voodoo who?
Voodoo you think you are?

Knock Knock
Who's there?
Vaughan!
Vaughan who?
Vaughan day you'll let me in!

Knock Knock
Who's there?
Vault!
Vault who?
(sings) Vault-sing Matilda!

Knock Knock
Who's there?
Willube!
Willube who?
Will you be my valentine?

Knock Knock
Who's there?
Witches!
Witches who?
Witches the way home?

Knock Knock
Who's there?
Water!
Water who?
What are friends for!

Knock Knock
Who's there?
William!
William who?
William mind your own business?

Knock Knock
Who's there?
Wafer!
Wafer who?
Wafer a long time but I'm back now!

Knock Knock
Who's there?
Woodward!
Woodward who?
Woodward would have come but
he was busy!

Knock Knock
Who's there?
Welcome!
Welcome who?
Welcome outside and join me!

Knock Knock
Who's there?
Wicked!
Wicked who?
Wicked be a great couple
if you gave me a chance!

Knock Knock
Who's there?
Wednesday!
Wednesday who?
(sings) Wednesday saints
go marching in!

Knock Knock
Who's there?
Who!
Who who?
What are you – an owl?

Knock Knock
Who's there?
Winner!
Winner who?
Winner you gonna get this door fixed?

Knock Knock
Who's there?
Weed!
Weed who?
Weed better mow the lawn
before it gets too long!

Knock Knock
Who's there?
Weirdo!
Weirdo who?
Weirdo you think you're going?

Knock Knock
Who's there?
Wilma!
Wilma who?
Wilma dinner be ready soon?

Knock Knock
Who's there?
Wanda!
Wanda who?
Wanda buy some cookies?

Knock Knock
Who's there?
Wayne!
Wayne who?
Wayne, wayne, go away,
come again another day!

Knock Knock
Who's there?
Watson!
Watson who?
Watson TV tonight?

Knock Knock
Who's there?
Waddle!
Waddle who?
Waddle you give me to leave you alone?

Knock Knock
Who's there?
Wenceslas!
Wenceslas who?
Wenceslas bus home?

Knock Knock
Who's there?
Who!
Who who?
I can hear an echo!

Knock Knock
Who's there?
Waiter!
Waiter who?
Waiter minute while I tie my shoe!

Knock Knock
Who's there?
Wooden shoe!
Wooden shoe who?
Wooden shoe like to know!

Knock Knock
Who's there?
X!
X who?
X-tremely pleased to meet you!

Knock Knock
Who's there?
X!
X who?
X for breakfast!

Knock Knock
Who's there?
Xavier!
Xavier who?
Xavier money for a rainy day!

Knock Knock
Who's there?
Xavier!
Xavier who?
Xavier breath, I'm
not leaving!

I'm allowed to change my mind... So I have! I'm leaving again!

Knock Knock
Who's there?
Xena!
Xena who?
Xena minute!

Knock Knock
Who's there?
Xenia!
Xenia who?
Xenia stealing my candy!

Knock Knock
Who's there?
Yah!
Yah who?
Ride 'em cowboy!

Knock Knock
Who's there?
You!
You who?
Did you call?

Knock Knock
Who's there?
Yul!
Yul who?
Yul never guess!

Knock Knock
Who's there?
Zombies!
Zombies who?
Zombies make honey, zombies just buzz around!

Knock Knock
Who's there?
Zany!
Zany who?
Zany body home?